ANIMAL IDIOMS

Strong as an Ox:
Are Oxen Powerful?

BY MATT LILLEY

CONTENT CONSULTANT
ANTHONY SEYKORA, PhD
PROFESSOR OF ANIMAL SCIENCE
UNIVERSITY OF MINNESOTA

Kids Core

An Imprint of Abdo Publishing
abdobooks.com

abdobooks.com

Published by Abdo Publishing, a division of ABDO, PO Box 398166, Minneapolis, Minnesota 55439. Copyright © 2022 by Abdo Consulting Group, Inc. International copyrights reserved in all countries. No part of this book may be reproduced in any form without written permission from the publisher. Kids Core™ is a trademark and logo of Abdo Publishing.

Printed in the United States of America, North Mankato, Minnesota.
102021
012022

THIS BOOK CONTAINS RECYCLED MATERIALS

Cover Photo: Wandel Guides/Shutterstock Images
Interior Photos: Shutterstock Images, 4–5, 6 (sky), 8, 12, 16–17, 18, 28 (bottom), 29 (top); Richard Griffin/Shutterstock Images, 6 (plant); Egasit Mullakhut/Shutterstock Images, 10–11; Elisabeth Aardema/Shutterstock Images, 14; Mircea Costina/Shutterstock Images, 20; Adam Reck/Shutterstock Images, 21; iStockphoto, 22, 23, 29 (bottom); Hung Chung Chih/Shutterstock Images, 24; Jan Schneckenhaus/Shutterstock Images, 25; Bernardo Emanuelle/Shutterstock Images, 26; Amanda Lewis/iStockphoto, 28 (top)

Editor: Christine Ha
Series Designer: Katharine Hale

Library of Congress Control Number: 2021941191

Publisher's Cataloging-in-Publication Data

Names: Lilley, Matt, author.
Title: Strong as an ox: are oxen powerful? / by Matt Lilley
Other title: are oxen powerful?
Description: Minneapolis, Minnesota : Abdo Publishing, 2022 | Series: Animal idioms | Includes online resources and index.
Identifiers: ISBN 9781532196713 (lib. bdg.) | ISBN 9781644946503 (pbk.) | ISBN 9781098218522 (ebook)
Subjects: LCSH: Oxen--Juvenile literature. | Cattle--Behavior--Juvenile literature. | Muscle strength--Juvenile literature. | Animal instinct--Juvenile literature. | Idiomatic expressions--Juvenile literature.
Classification: DDC 599.735--dc23

CONTENTS

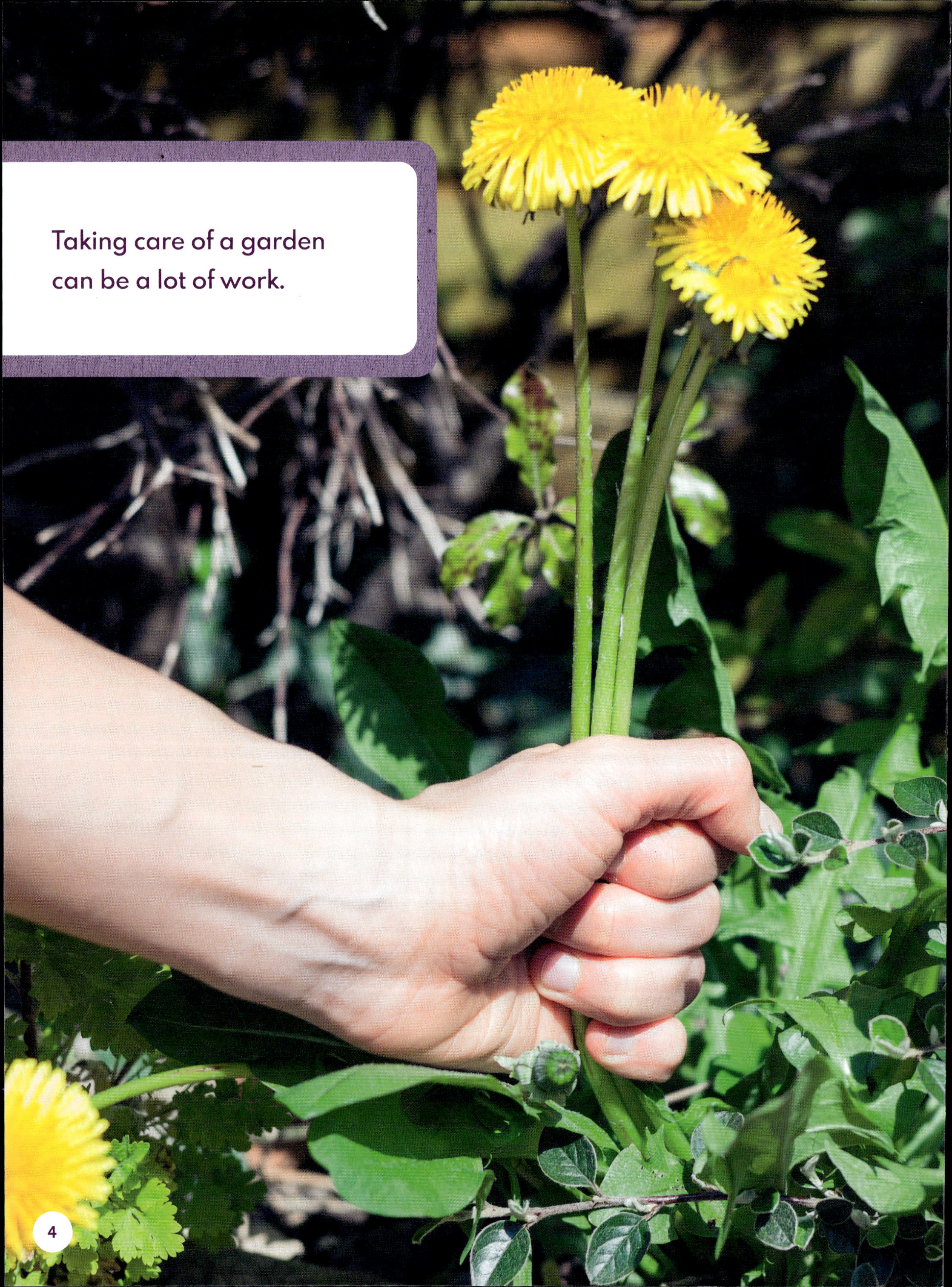

Taking care of a garden can be a lot of work.

CHAPTER 1

How Strong?

Sophia and Tashi were outside gardening and pulling up weeds. Sophia struggled to pull up a big one. She tugged and tugged, but it would not budge. "Tashi, can you help pull this one?"

Sometimes weeds can be hard to remove. Their roots have grown deep into the soil.

"Don't worry! I've got it!" Tashi grabbed the weed. She yanked it up with one hand, roots and all.

Sophia's mouth dropped. She said, "Whoa! You are as strong as an ox!"

"Hey! Take it back!" Tashi demanded. "I'm not an ox!"

"I didn't say you are an ox. I said you're as strong as an ox! That's really strong!" Sophia flexed her muscles.

Tashi smiled. "I'll take that as a compliment then!" Before long, Tashi and Sophia finished pulling all the weeds.

What Are Idioms?

Strong as an ox is an idiom. An idiom is an expression that is often used in a specific language. Sophia compared Tashi to an ox. She doesn't really think Tashi is like an ox. She just means that Tashi is very strong.

A Is for Ox?

The letter *A* came from the ancient Egyptian writing symbol in the shape of an ox's head. Some language experts believe people put the letter *A* at the beginning of the alphabet to honor the strength and helpfulness of the ox.

Oxen are big animals. They usually weigh between 1,500 and 3,000 pounds (680 and 1,360 kg).

Are oxen really strong? While idioms are not always true, *strong as an ox* is based on the truth. Oxen are cattle that have been trained to do work. Oxen are strong. They help humans do a lot of hard jobs. Humans have used them for thousands of years. Oxen have even helped shape history with the work they have done.

Explore Online

Visit the website below. Does it give any new information about idioms?

Why Do People Use Idioms?

abdocorelibrary.com/strong-as-an-ox

Oxen have been important in cultures around the world.

CHAPTER 2

Humans and Oxen

Cattle is another name for cows. Humans first **domesticated** cattle about 10,500 years ago. People kept these first cattle for their meat and milk. **Archaeologists** believe cattle were first trained to do work about 6,000 years ago. These working cattle were oxen.

A benefit of using oxen for work is that oxen can move through mud and snow better than horses.

In many different cultures, oxen were the **beasts of burden**. This meant that their strength was used to carry heavy loads.

They could also perform difficult tasks such as plowing.

The plows oxen pulled turned over and loosened the soil. Plowing also uprooted weeds to keep them from growing over crops. This made land good for crops like corn and wheat. An ox let one farmer work ten times more land than before. This meant more people were fed in the farmer's family or community.

Earth Shaker

Oxen can be found in **mythology** around the world. In a legend from the Gansu province of China, there is an ox so strong that it carries the entire earth on its back. When annoyed, it shakes and causes earthquakes.

Beef and dairy are still important foods for humans to this day.

Farms became much bigger and produced more food. Cattle also became a steady source of food. More food led to more people, and cities grew bigger.

Oxen also changed the way many people lived. The animals took over the hardest work on farms. People no longer had to work as hard. They could focus on new kinds of work, such as art, building, or metalworking. Many people turned to other jobs.

Further Evidence

Look at the website below. Does it give any new evidence to support Chapter Two?

Cows

abdocorelibrary.com/strong-as-an-ox

The use of oxen is still very common in South America, Central America, and Asia.

CHAPTER 3

What It Takes to Be an Ox

To this day, many farmers prefer oxen over machines or other technology. Farming machines like tractors and plows are often expensive. Oxen are cheaper and live around 20 years.

Cattle can be many sizes and colors. They may also be with or without horns.

They eat cheap food like grain instead of running on more expensive fuels like gasoline. They can also go across many different kinds of land and do all types of work.

There are more than 900 kinds of cattle. Any type of cattle can be trained to be oxen. But dairy cows are often used. Dairy cows are cattle used for their milk. Farmers prefer to train calm cows that get along with humans. Since dairy cows are around humans often, they are usually easy to handle.

It takes years of training for cattle to become oxen. Training starts when the cattle are just a few months old. Trained oxen know how to do work. They also know how to follow directions.

By the time a cow in training reaches 6 to 12 months old, it usually has already learned basic commands.

Oxen working together are called a team. The person who tells a team of oxen what to do is called either a drover or a teamster. Oxen watch the drover for hand signals. They also listen to voice commands. Oxen are taught commands to turn, slow down, move forward and backward, stop, and go.

Drovers often hold a long stick to tap an ox to tell it to move, stop, speed up, or slow down.

Yokes are custom-made for each ox or team of oxen. New yokes may need to be made as the oxen get bigger.

To do work, oxen are put in a yoke. A yoke is a beam of wood that holds oxen together. Over long distances, a team of oxen can pull its own body weight. Over short distances, a team can pull up to 13,000 pounds (5,900 kg).

Oxen and Yokes

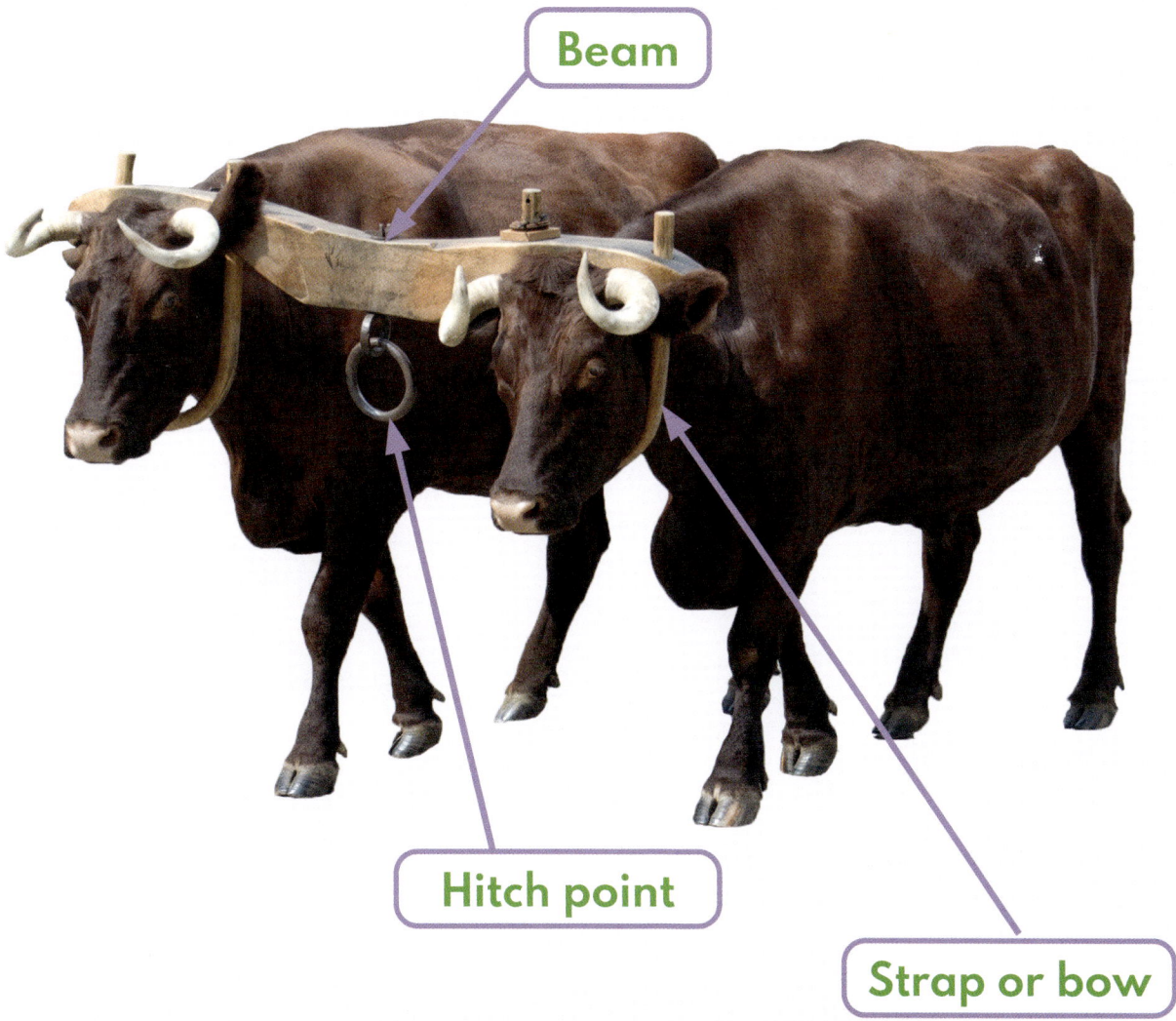

Beam

Hitch point

Strap or bow

Oxen are often put on yokes to help them pull heavy loads.
Yokes are designed so that the pulling force goes through the
oxen's shoulders.

A common job that oxen help with is pulling farmers' heavy plows.

Most work for oxen involves pulling heavy loads. They can pull different kinds of farm machines. They can pull plows to prepare fields,

Sometimes, oxen are used to draw carts or wagons for transportation.

rake hay, or clear snow. They can pull logs for lumberjacks. They can pull wagons for travel.

Oxen Horns

Most oxen have horns so yokes will not slip off their heads. For example, when they are pulling something down a hill, they might have to slow down. They brake by pushing back against the yokes with their horns.

Lighter tasks, like carting smaller equipment, can use just one ox.

Oxen have great **endurance**. They can work for a long time and not get tired. While oxen are not fast, they are strong and steady. Oxen are hard workers that combine strength and intelligence.

Journalist Sue Bowman learned about ox training from a couple of New York farmers:

> "A young steer will progress through several stages of [ability], including 'clever steer,' 'handy steer' and 'working steer' before earning designation as ox. . . . some calves will . . . fail to achieve status as oxen."

Source: Sue Bowman. "Oxen No Has-Beens When It Comes to Hard Pulling." *Lancaster Farming*, 29 Oct. 2011, lancasterfarming.com. Accessed 30 June 2021.

What's the Big Idea?

Read the article carefully. What is its main idea? Explain how the main idea is supported by details, naming 2 or 3 of those supporting details.

Ox Facts

Cattle were first domesticated by humans about 10,500 years ago. Some were used for work. Working cattle are called oxen.

It takes cattle several years to train to be oxen.

A team of oxen can pull up to 13,000 pounds (5,900 kg) for short distances.

Oxen have a lot of endurance. They can work for a long time without getting tired.

Glossary

archaeologists
scientists who study human history and culture by examining things people made, used, and left behind

beasts of burden
animals, such as oxen and horses, that are used to perform difficult work

domesticated
changed from a wild plant or animal to one that can live alongside humans

endurance
the ability to work hard for a long time

mythology
a culture's traditional stories that explain the world in some way

Online Resources

To learn more about oxen, visit our free resource websites below.

Core Library CONNECTION
FREE! COMMON CORE MULTIMEDIA RESOURCES

Visit **abdocorelibrary.com** or scan this QR code for free Common Core resources for teachers and students, including vetted activities, multimedia, and booklinks, for deeper subject comprehension.

Booklinks NONFICTION NETWORK
FREE! ONLINE NONFICTION RESOURCES

Visit **abdobooklinks.com** or scan this QR code for free additional online weblinks for further learning. These links are routinely monitored and updated to provide the most current information available.

Learn More

Byard, Jack. *Know Your Cows*. Old Pond Publishing, 2020.

Lilley, Matt. *Stubborn as a Mule*. Abdo, 2022.

Statts, Leo. *Cows*. Abdo, 2017.

Index

About the Author

Matt Lilley is the author of more than a dozen books for children. He holds a master's in scientific and technical writing from the University of Minnesota. He has also worked as an elementary school literacy tutor for Reading Corps, a division of AmeriCorps. He lives in Minnesota with his family.